funky
JUNK

funky JUNK

fresh ideas to jazz up your junk

HarperCollins Publishers

To the best kids ever – Roxy, Roo and Leo – the Walton All Stars

First published in 1999 by HarperCollins*Publishers*
in association with Granada Television Limited

Text © 1999 Stewart & Sally Walton
Design, layout and specially commissioned photography
© HarperCollins*Publishers*

A catalogue record for this book is available from the British Library.
ISBN 000 414 096 6

Editor: Antonia Maxwell
Designer: Kathryn Gammon
Photographer: Steven Differ

Cover picture credits: front cover, main image Simon Kenny/Arcaid.
All other photographs Steven Differ

Additional picture credits:
Abode: *24-5, 26, 27b, 28-9, 34, 35, 38, 39t,b, 43b, 44-5, 46-7*
Arcaid: *Earl Carter 40b, 41, 43t; Simon Kenny 36, 40t; Weidland 27m;*
Alan Weintraub 6, 8-9, 32b, 33, 37, 42
Britstock-IFA: *17, 21, 82-3, 84b*
Camera Press: *2, 14-15, 31t, 84t, 86b, 87, 92b*
DIY Photo library: *84m, 85b, 86tl, r, c, 88t, 89, 90b, 91l, r, 92t, 93*
Elizabeth Whiting & Associates: *22, 30, 31m, 88b*
Robert Harding Picture Library: *12, 16, 20, 85tl,tr*
r= right, l=left, t=top, b=bottom, m=middle

Colour reproduction by Colourscan, Singapore
Printed and bound in Italy

'Funky Junk' was produced for transmission on
Granada TV's 'This Morning' programme, September 1999

Presented by Stewart and Sally Walton
Produced and directed by Jane Gerber
Researcher: Joanna Bennet-Coles
Series Editor: Helen Williams

contents

looking for junk

funky junk is not valuable, but it is precious; it may not cost much, but it is priceless. It is *your* thing – unlike anyone else's and that's why you like it.

Once you choose the funky route all other paths will seem dull. You will become an expert at peeling off layers of paint, pulling out twisted nails, stripping off decorations, and, most of all, at spotting potential. It could be the curve of a table leg, the shape of a mirror, or the generous proportions of an armchair. You will spurn perfection in favour of promise, and, like a talent scout, you will have to reject a lot of contenders before you find your star.

Junk is for people who have more time than money. If you have unlimited funds you can shop at places where people with fabulous taste sell furniture and objects of great individuality and style. If you work all week and have limited time to shop for furniture, you may end up in a store buying the style of the

A flea-market is junk heaven and the ideal place to rescue unwanted items in need of funk.

moment and, if you're not careful, living in a home that resembles a showroom in a furniture store. Getting funky with junk will soon rectify that.

It makes far more sense to buy an old, wooden piece of furniture in need of repair than a characterless new piece made out of fibreboard. It is hard to imagine today's mass-produced furniture lasting long enough to fill the junk shops of the future. Only at the top end of the market are things made to last.

One way of injecting a bit of eclectic style into your home is through inherited furniture – not priceless antiques, although they would be nice, but ordinary household furniture that elderly relatives are inclined to throw out in favour of something easier to keep clean and move about. Those lovely old wooden garden chairs can vanish overnight to be replaced by moulded plastic ones unless you make your wishes clear.

We are not suggesting that you prey on the elderly, but we know from personal experience that it is often the thing we like best in our aunts' and grandparents' homes that they actually like the least and throw on the bonfire. Our advice is to be sensitively ruthless and stake your claim politely.

We once lived in a street where one of our neighbours had a flourishing dual career as both manager of the local household rubbish dump and bric-a-brac dealer in London's Portobello Road antiques market. Following his lead, we all rapidly became a street full of junk fiends. There was soon no junk shop unvisited, no garage sale unattended and no roadside skip uninvestigated. We would hire stalls in charity markets just to have the first look at the other stallholder's stock, and would usually have spent more than we could hope to make long

Before and after: it's amazing what a lick of paint can do!

before the doors were opened to the public. That was twenty years ago and we have yet to find an antidote. Be warned!

The seaside town where we now live is the closest thing to junk heaven you could find, with all levels catered for, from tiny antique shops to large communal flea markets and weekend charity markets where people turn up with their cars loaded and sell their unwanted possessions to each other at knock-down prices, usually departing in cars still full, but with other people's junk.

We hope that this book will inspire you to start snooping around your locality in search of furniture with potential that you can make over. If you are a novice, then charity shops and markets, jumble sales and garage sales are the best places to start because everyone is involved on an amateur level. People get rid of things for many different reasons, not

Prams, busts, trunks, mirrors, signs, globes, boats, hip-flasks – many surprises await you!

16

just because they are worn out or broken. We have found some of our favourite pieces at table sales in muddy fields, including a strap iron gate, and a delicate Chinese silk bed cover.

It is a good idea to pay regular visits to local second-hand furniture dealers. This way you become familiar with their stock and will soon be able to spot any new additions. You also get to know the traders and develop an idea of the type of things they are likely to buy for resale. If you have something particular in mind, a wooden standard lamp for instance, a dealer would be happy to save you the time and footwork by keeping a lookout for one on your behalf. Many traders enjoy getting to know their customers and predicting the sort of things that will appeal to them.

Markets present a different sort of challenge. You need to be bold and decisive and able to spot potential at a glance without appearing more than mildly interested. Play at being cautious and see how negotiable the price is. Haggling is all part of the fun for both the stall holder and the buyer, and a successful outcome is one where you have seen the price drop sufficiently to make you feel you have got a bargain, and the trader has not dropped it far enough to wipe out their profit margin. It is a mutually satisfying game.

Auction sales offer great potential for both bargain hunters and thrill seekers. Choose a small auction where the lots are mostly household items and unlikely to attract the interest of professional antique dealers. Every auction has a catalogue of the num-

Never pass a charity shop without popping in – they are a great source of bargain finds.

bered lots, and there will be a viewing period before the auction begins, giving the buyers a chance to see the lots

Regular markets have a quick turnover, so don't hesitate if you spot something you like.

at close quarters and check on their condition. It is a good idea to set yourself a price limit and mark the catalogue accordingly. When the bidding starts, it is all to easy to get carried away with the competition and pay too much, but if you have already decided on a top limit, you may avoid overspending. Once the auction's excitement is over, you will have to remove your purchases from the premises, so bear this in mind if you feel tempted to bid for a large wardrobe! Auction houses do arrange delivery but usually at a premium.

Once you have bought your junk, the fun really starts. Try not to look on repair work as a chore; half of the fun of buying old stuff instead of new is that you have the opportunity to delve into its past, peeling off old layers and finding

out about the way it was made. The ultimate satisfaction is in seeing it brought back to life.

In this book, we have explained the different techniques we used in the actual projects, and there is also a more general section on materials and techniques at the end of the book.

The emphasis is on having fun rather than on serious restoration, but we have still spent time on repairs and preparation and hope that the book will prove instructional as well as inspirational. We have chosen a wide range of objects and have been able to cover a variety of different approaches and use different techniques. There are two main starting points when doing up junk: either you go out and find something and see what it suggests to you, or you have a technique in mind and go shopping for something on which you can experiment.

When planning these projects we set ourselves very strict rules: everything chosen had to be genuine junk, and there was to be no cheating by starting off with something halfway decent. We never use pieces of real quality.

Over the past decade, several popular television programmes on the subject of antiques have made the general public far more aware of their value, both in monetary and historical terms. The upside of this is that beautiful objects are no longer destroyed on a fashion whim; the downside is that we are all far less likely to find a genuine antique when hunting for junk.

If you do find something of quality, then you will have the chance to do some detective work. Most makers of fine furniture, china, silverware or glass will have left their mark somewhere on their work. Libraries have reference books that

list identification marks, or you can ask a reputable antiques dealer for an opinion. Bear in mind though that dealers all have their eye on the main chance, and be wary if they offer to take something off your hands – it may be a rare and valuable find!

If you find a genuine antique which does not appeal to your personal taste, resist giving it a funky makeover. Respect the craftsmanship of the piece, even if you do not like the style, and offer it for resale through a dealer, or pass it on to someone who you know will love it.

We hope that *Funky Junk* will inspire everyone who reads it to have a go at one or two of the projects, and that for some it will be the start of a whole new lifestyle involving exciting finds, highly individual makeovers and a new awareness of junk's potential. Our aim has been to wave a funky magic wand and grant some style wishes to deserving but neglected bits and pieces, by adding colour, pattern, texture and a good helping of humour.

Enjoy the process as much as the result, and always feel free to make changes by injecting a bit of your own funky attitude to give your work a style of its own.

Reclamation yards are great sources of tiles, handles and other accessories.

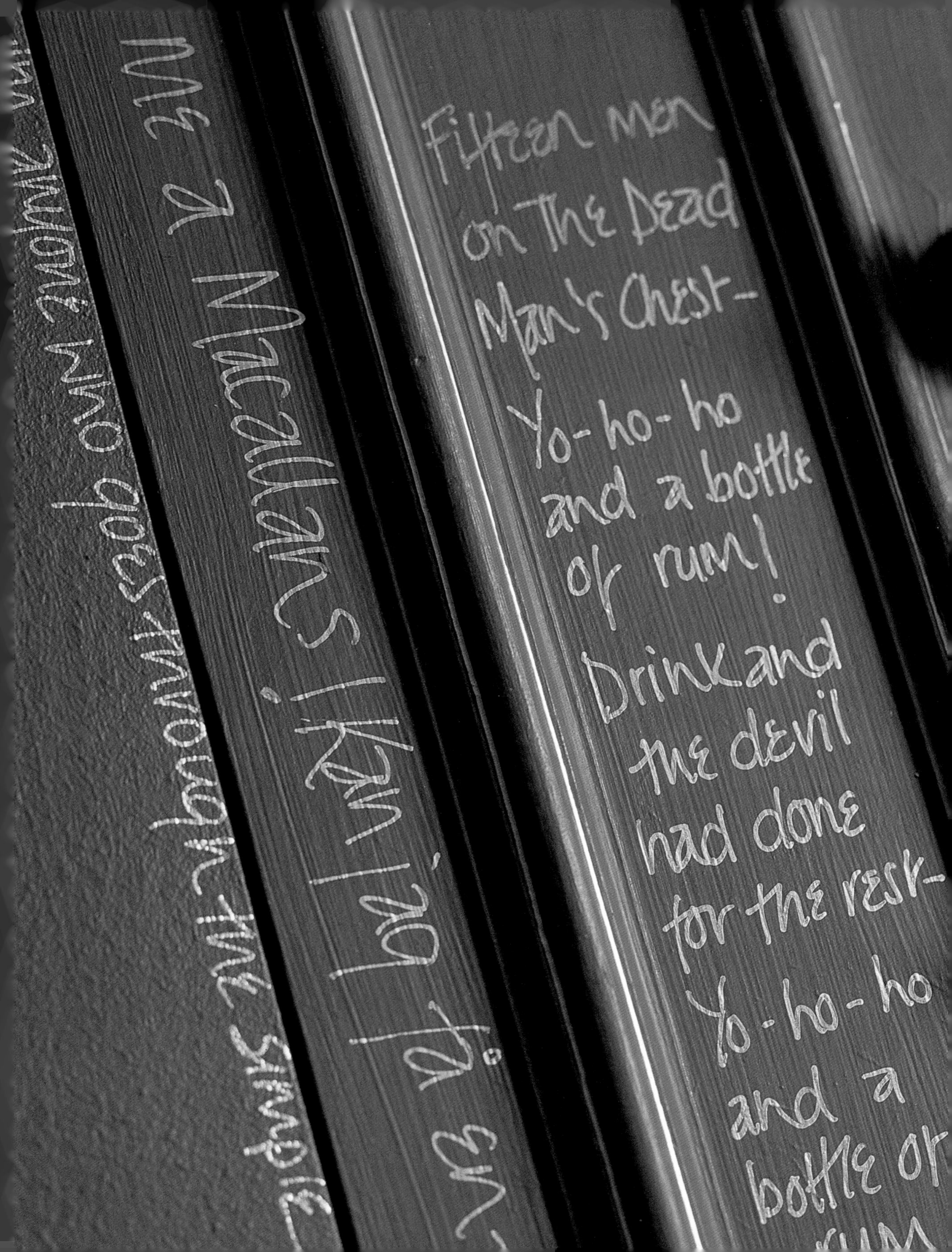

Fifteen men
on The Dead
Man's Chest—

Yo-ho-ho
and a bottle
of rum!

Drink and
the devil
had done
for the rest—

Yo-ho-ho
and a
bottle or
rum

Me 2 Macallans | Keh '20 -

no one goes through the simple

inspirations

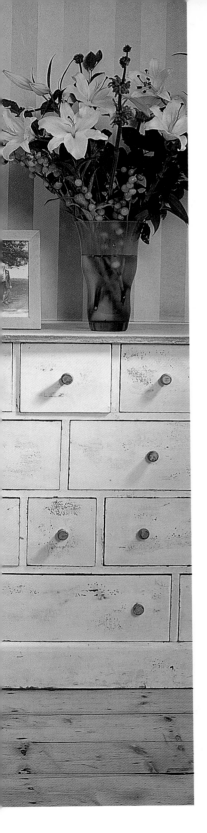

Funky furniture

Large items of furniture are often the most expensive to buy new, so they are an ideal place to start funking up your junk. We suggest you start by looking at what you already have – paint, paper and a bit of imagination can make a little potential go a long way!

stylish storage

If your cupboards need a new lease of life, or you find a bargain old pine dresser or shelf, you can jazz it up to make it fit into your home. The cupboard on the left has been painted with a rich purple emulsion and then decorated using a metallic gold pen. With a coat of varnish it will last for ages. Anything goes, and it needn't cost the earth.

Funky chairs

Old chairs always seem to be better made than their modern contemporaries. If you have or find an old chair, a paint job and some new upholstery can work wonders.

Beautiful bedrooms

There are some amazing beds and other pieces of furniture to be found at antique fairs and salvage yards around the country. Even paying for a professional welder to make essential repairs may still leave you with something a bit special and for far less than the cost of mass-produced furniture.

All wrapped up!

In this room, old sheets
of music have been used
in place of wallpaper.
You could use the same
techniques with newspapers
(a particular birthday?),
funky wrapping paper or
old comics – check that
they aren't valuable first!

Lighting

Think laterally when looking for junk lighting. You may be lucky enough to find a wonderful old lamp that just needs a good clean, but don't automatically reject the lamp that is missing a base or fitting. If you find something with a beautiful shade or upright, keep it and carry on looking until you find something to go with it.

Funky frames

The imagination really is
the only limit to what you
can use as a frame.
Here, old frames have
been revarnished and
painted to give them a
new life. We include
some ideas later in the
book for Funky Frames,
so let your imagination
run riot!

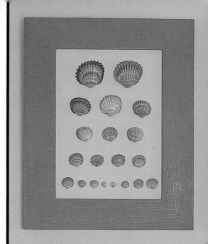

Just junk

Junk for junk's sake – this is the very best kind of funky junk! A collection of groovy hats, or shells or even colanders, as shown here, can look amazing. The trick is to think about display – who needs art?

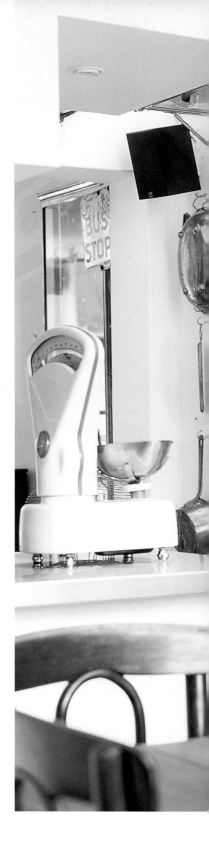

42

More
memorabilia

Gather together your
favourite collections or
photographs – junk
displayed together
creates quite an impact.

Kitchen craft

There are always plenty
of old plates and other
assorted pieces of
crockery in car-boot sales
and junk shops. Nothing
ever matches – so why
not bring them together
using your own design?
Use ceramic paints to
transform old-fashioned
crockery into a
contemporary and
unique collection.

Jazz it up!

Terracotta plant pots are inexpensive and available at large garden centres. You can also find them in junk shops, or you may find some at the bottom of your garden! A lick of paint can ring the changes, and you can also bring them indoors as colourful containers for houseplants.

Painted tiles are ideal for transforming old tables – you can buy tiles you particularly like (below right), or paint old or inexpensive ones (above right) to your own taste. See our tiled table later in the book for how to do-it-yourself.

the makeovers

MARRIAGE WITN

funky furniture

fernwork wardrobe

Fernwork is a treatment for woodwork which was first popular in Victorian times. Using real leaves as templates to block the colour in places, paint is sprayed on and when the leaves are removed their shadow shapes remain. These days spray mount and car spray make this project one of the easiest ways to make a funky statement.

We picked our ferns from the wild, but you could cheat and use fakes – the plastic ones have very realistic shapes and will give the same effect with no risk of breaking up. Be creative! Choose bold colours for maximum impact and create a fern frenzy. Choose a wardrobe that is constructed from solid wood, checking that the hinges work. Avoid any with really musty odours as these are hard to get rid of.

you will need:

- 1 large double-door wardrobe ▪ electric sander (or sandpaper and elbow grease!)
- white spirit and cloth ▪ white acrylic primer
- small foam rollers and tray ▪ basecoat emulsion ▪ fern leaves – real or fake – or any other leaves with well-defined shapes such as palm fronds ▪ spray mount ▪ 3 cans of car spray paint – our colour is cobalt blue ▪ safety mask ▪ clear satin varnish and clean brush

Preparing the leaves

If your leaves are freshly picked they will need to be flattened. Arrange them between sheets of newspaper and place a board on top with a couple of bricks as weights. Leave them for a day or two. Do not allow them to dry out too much as they will become crumbly.

1 Sand your wardrobe to prepare the surface and give the paint something to key into. Use the small roller to apply a coat of primer. This paint is quick-drying and, if you feel it will need more than one coat, the second can be applied an hour later.

2 Next comes the basecoat. We used a bright primrose-yellow emulsion, applied with a small roller. Rollers are usually sold in packs with three spares, and it is best to use a new one for each change of colour.

3 Once the basecoat has dried, select a few large ferns to make up the main pattern. Then fill in the spaces with smaller ferns. Lift each fern, spray the back with spray mount and replace it, trying not to move it about as that will affect the finish of the paint.

4 Put on the face mask and apply the aerosol paint. Keep an even pressure and build up the colour gradually. Start with a light covering and work within your arm's reach. Aim for an even depth of colour, and make sure all areas are blended together.

5 Leave until the paint is completely dry. Lift the ferns to reveal their shadow shapes in the contrasting basecoat colour.

6 Once you have lifted all the ferns, apply a coat of clear matt varnish with a clean brush. This will add years of life to your funky fernwork.

patchwork tile table

This little table looked dowdy and neglected when we found it under a pile of old furniture in a second-hand store. The legs were solid wood but the Formica top had begun to lift from its wooden base, so we decided it would be better to completely remove it and give it a funky new look.

We decided to tile the table top using a box of brightly coloured 'seconds' and, as some were chipped, we had to cut some of the tiles in half diagonally, some horizontally and some vertically. Once we had enough to cover the table top we reassembled them to make a vibrant, colourful patchwork pattern. Tiles are very easy to cut, and mixing up shapes and colours gives a really dynamic effect. The pale table legs needed a bit of drama, so we rolled on a coat of blackboard paint to give them a sexy opaque matt finish.

you will need:

- table ▪ hammer and chisel ▪ electric sander (or sandpaper and elbow grease!) ▪ white spirit and cloth ▪ tile cutter ▪ ceramic tiles in variety of colours – enough to cover the table top
- tile adhesive and grout ▪ grouting trowel
- matt black emulsion or blackboard paint
- sponge roller

1 Using the hammer and chisel, lift the old Formica surface from the wooden table top. Be careful of the sharp edges and try not to dig the chisel into the wood. It should come off as a single sheet.

2 Sand away the old gloss paint using an electric sander, if you have one. If not use sandpaper. Wipe the table legs down with a cloth dampened with white spirit to get rid of the dust and any greasy marks that will repel the new paint.

3 A tile cutter is quite easy to use. The tile is placed in the cutter and a line is scratched on the surface to cut through the glaze. Move the cutter to the top of the tile and press down. The tile will snap along the scratched line.

4 Plan your patchwork pattern and then place to one side. Apply a 1cm/¼-in layer of tile adhesive to the table top and arrange the tiles on it. Push them into the adhesive, leaving a small gap between them.

5 Leave the adhesive to set and apply the tile grout. Grout is usually sold with an applicator, but we used a grouting trowel which made the job even easier. Once the grout had dried we wiped the tiles with a damp sponge and buffed them up with a duster.

6 We left the black paint until last (in case the grouting dripped) and applied it with a sponge roller. The table looked absolutely brilliant with its shiny trim and drawer back in place, proving that there is life for junk after Formica!

sugar candy cradle

If you've always envied people who have wonderful family heirlooms, remember that they had to begin somewhere. Second-hand cradles abound because many, many babies can sleep in them before they show any signs of wear and tear, but everyone wants their first baby to have something individual and wonderful all of their own.

For this project we fixed up an old, rickety cradle, painting it in soft sugared-almond colours before adding the new baby's name.

This old cot really had seen better days, but the shape was basically good and we knew it could be made safe, secure and totally irresistible.

After stripping and priming we painted the cot with satinwood paint which is tough, oil-based and dries to a soft sheen. We chose pastel pink, yellow, cream and blue for the cot, but brighter versions of the same colours would give the cot a real Caribbean look.

The cot was given a new mattress covered with a totally funky fabric bought from a charity shop. Always buy a new mattress for a second-hand cradle or cot.

you will need:
- second-hand cot or cradle ■ hammer
- paint stripper, scraper and rubber gloves
- wire wool ■ sandpaper ■ aerosol primer and face mask ■ 3 or more colours of satinwood paint ■ paint brushes or contour surface pads for painting spindles ■ artist's brushes for the lettering ■ new foam mattress ■ fabric and elastic for the cover

1 Remove any broken pieces and pull out all protruding nails. Each cradle or cot will be different, but it is of utmost importance to make yours safe. Dismantle the cradle, which makes it easier to work with.

2 Cover the work area. Then, wearing rubber gloves, coat the old paint with a generous amount of paint stripper and leave it until the paint begins to crinkle. Remove the paint using a scraper.

3 Remove any stubborn paint by rubbing it with wire wool. Use sandpaper to smooth the wood and to prepare the surface for painting. Take the cradle pieces outside, and spray evenly with primer.

4 Apply the paint. Use a different
brush or contour surface pad for each
colour and change the colour for each
spindle. The frame could be one colour
and the rockers another. Add the
baby's name in a contrasting colour.

Safety advice

- *Old paint may contain lead which is very hazardous, especially
to babies and young children. We suggest you buy a lead-testing
kit before you scrape off any paint. If the paint does contain lead
you can have it professionally dipped in a caustic solution to
remove the paint thoroughly.*

- *Always use rubber gloves when using paint stripper and work
in a well-ventilated area – preferably outside.*

57

mexican dressing table

We took our inspiration from Mexican folk-art, where everything is painted and patterned in a riot of colour and energetically decorated with punched tin cans and bottle caps. The attitude needed here is bold, so risk being a bit sloppy with the paint as you work fast and furiously.

We stripped our dressing table bare and painted it using a mixture of a vibrant colours. Once this had dried we painted patterns free-hand using a fat brush, and then made foil stars to embellish the handles. The top was completely covered with bottle caps giving it a jewel-bright surface.

you will need:
- dressing table or sideboard ■ sandpaper
- white spirit and a cloth ■ wire wool and metal cleaner ■ 4 brightly coloured emulsion paints ■ heavyweight metal foil from a craft materials supplier ■ scissors ■ tracing wheel or pastry cutter ■ pencil ■ brightly coloured artist's acrylic paints ■ metal bottle caps – ask a friendly barman to save them for you, or throw a party! ■ strong contact adhesive
- PVA glue and stiff brush

1 Prepare the woodwork by rubbing it down with sandpaper to remove all the old polish and varnish.

2 Dampen a cloth with white spirit and use it to wipe off the dust and remove any greasy marks.

3 Before you start painting, clean up any metalwork that cannot be removed and refitted. These drawer handles were riveted in place and looked bright and shiny after a rub with wire wool and metal cleaner.

4 We painted the frame and top ultramarine blue, and the drawers lime green, yellow and Indian red. We used a mixture of the colours for the uprights, mirror frame and sides of the dressing table. Leave to dry.

5 To make the foil stars, cut the metal with scissors, and mark patterns on the reverse side with a biro. To add a wavy dotted line, use a tracing wheel. We decorated the paintwork with wild squiggles, zig-zags, swirls and brush prints and some bold woodgraining.

6 The bottle caps were stuck down in rows using strong contact adhesive and the foil stars were glued on with PVA. It is hard to know when to stop when you are going over the top like this – sundown perhaps?

gilded thrones

We fell in love with the regal shape of these armchairs and decided that they would make a perfect pair of thrones. Their transformation began with the drab dark-blue paintwork being rubbed down and replaced by fresh coats of mulberry-pink and jade-green emulsion paint.

We wanted to give them a glamourous but contemporary look, and applied gold and silver leaf randomly to the arms and seats. Some of the paint colour shows through the cracks in the leaf, and to accentuate this two-tone effect, we masked off a star pattern on the seat and spots on the arms.

This technique should not be confused with traditional gilding which is a highly specialised craft involving complex recipes for the glue called 'size', hours of preparation with gesso and bole, and delicate timing for the seamless application of the precious leaf. The finish is as near to real gold or silver as you can imagine. Our method is a lot more fun, much quicker, and definitely more funky.

you will need:
- 2 wooden chairs – carvers from a dining suite are perfect • medium-grade sandpaper • sugar soap and a sponge • 2 or more colours of emulsion paint • 2 sponge rollers with trays
- coins and strips of paper • spray mount
- gold and silver leaf – Dutch metal and aluminium leaf are cheap substitutes • soft cloth • clear matt varnish and new brush

1 Rub off the top coat of paint or varnish using medium-grade sandpaper. Mix the sugar soap according to directions and sponge the chairs with it.

2 Paint the chairs with the emulsion paint. A small sponge roller is the easiest way to apply emulsion paint to furniture as it is quick and allows for an even application.

3 When the paint is dry, place two coins on each of the arms. These will mask the surface and appear as dots of colour through the gilded arms. Cut scrap paper into strips about 2.5cm/ 1in wide and 25cm/10in long.

4 Arrange the strips of paper on the seats, intersecting to form star shapes. Place a coin on the end of each strip to keep it in place. Protect the floor area and apply a light coating of spray mount over the chair arms and seats. Leave the spray mount for five minutes then remove the coins and paper.

5 Take individual sheets of leaf and backing paper and lay them face down onto the sticky surfaces. Rub the backing paper lightly to transfer the leaf. Lift the sheets and use a soft cloth to burnish the leaf and rub away the adhesive where it was blocked by the coins and paper strips.

6 A final coat of clear varnish over the gilding and the emulsion will give the chairs a tough finish and and a glossy shine.

hall stand

This hall stand was made in the 1940s when materials were scarce, and drab was the only style option. Still, it survived and now it is having a moment of fame! We were instantly attracted to its eccentric shape, the oval mirror and the flat panels.

Maps and atlases that are out of date can be found in abundance. Their patterns and colours make wonderful decoupage material and the large ones can also be used as alternative wallpaper. At first we planned to restrict the maps to the panels on the hall stand, but as we worked we began to visualise how it would look covered entirely – so we went for it!

You will need:
- dresser ▪ screwdriver or electric drill
- sandpaper and cork sanding block
- white spirit and cloth ▪ brown paper
- scissors ▪ selection of old maps (old school atlases are not rare and can be cut up without guilt) ▪ wallpaper paste ▪ bucket
- old paintbrush ▪ varnish and a clean brush

1 Remove any fittings from your dresser. The screws that held the coat hooks in place on our hall stand had rusted so we used an electric drill to remove them.

3 Wipe the entire surface with a cloth that has been dampened with white spirit to remove any dust or grease marks. The white spirit evaporates from the surface leaving it clean, dry and ready to take wallpaper paste.

5 Mix the wallpaper paste and apply it over the hall stand using an old paint brush. Make sure that all mouldings and indents are covered, as well as the large flat panels.

2 Rub the hall stand down well with sandpaper to remove all traces of varnish. Use a medium- to hard-grade sandpaper on a cork sanding block for the large flat areas, and rolled-up sandpaper to get into any mouldings.

4 Use the brown paper to make templates for the maps. Smooth it against the hall stand and draw on the outlines of the panels. Draw around the templates onto the maps and cut around.

6 Paste the pieces of map and place them in position on the hall stand. Use the cloth to smooth any bubbles under the maps. Leave to dry completely and then varnish using a clean brush to protect the maps.

the love thing

Love, in this case, is pronounced *lurve*! The idea behind it was to have a special place to store mementoes, photographs and other precious reminders of what being in love is all about. It may be a silly note left on the kitchen table, a pressed flower from your wedding bouquet, or the key to your first front door.

We all need romance and sometimes, when life is hectic and the pressure is on, we can forget just how important love is. When you're feeling low, get 'the love thing' out for a five-minute stock-take to remind yourself of the good times. Then close the lid with a smile on your lips and a Barry White song in your heart! You know it makes sense.

We found this neglected and rusty chest in a flea market and gave it the love treatment, transforming it with cut-outs from the covers of cheap romantic novels, leopard-skin giftwrap, lace doilies, fake jewels and a lining of plush pink velvet. It's kitsch but it's cute, and it will make you smile.

you will need:
- selection of paperback romance novels with raunchy covers ■ animal-print giftwrap
- lace coasters or doilies ■ costume jewellery, tassels, silk cords or velvet flowers ■ scissors
- wire wool ■ white spirit and cloth
- wallpaper paste ■ PVA glue ■ glue gun and glue sticks ■ water-based matt varnish tinted with watercolour ink ■ sandpaper

1 Select the images for your collage. Book covers are usually too thick to bend smoothly over curves, and the images will be easier to work with if you make colour photocopies of your favourites. The colours may be considerably brighter and more garish when copied, but this isn't a bad thing.

2 Do any repairs to the chest that are needed. A metal chest will need to be rubbed down with wire wool to get rid of any rust. Wipe the surface with a cloth dampened with white spirit to remove any dust and grease spots.

3 Paint the surface of the chest with wallpaper paste. Cover the chest with sheets of giftwrap. Snip the paper to mould it around any protruding bits and the corners. Wallpaper paste makes paper stretch, but it pulls it tight and smooth as it dries.

4 Plan your basic layout by building up the background first and then adding the feature images. These can either be used centrally or alongside another image of the same scale. As this is a personal memoir you are bound to have your own ideas.

5 Paint on PVA glue and sprinkle with glitter to add further sparkle. Give the outside a rosy glow by applying several coats of tinted varnish. Sand between coats. We used a few drops of watercolour ink (Windsor & Newton's Process Magenta) to tint the varnish.

Finishing touches

With decoupage and collage you get a more cohesive effect as you add more coats of varnish until the surface becomes level. So if this is to be a real labour of love, and not just a passing fling, we suggest you varnish this 'love thing' ten times, rubbing it down lightly with fine sand-paper between coats.

giraffe trunk

Trunks are widely available and always useful, so do pick one up if you find one. This tin trunk was in good condition but it lacked soul, so we thought it would be fun to both warm it up and soften it down with an unusual paint finish. And what could be more naturally funky than a giraffe skin pattern?

A fascinating fact about giraffes is that each one has a different skin pattern. Quite incredible when you try to imagine that amount of variations of brownish squares on a cream background. For this project it means that you can't go wrong when painting the giraffe skin pattern – it is bound to match up with a giraffe somewhere!

You will need:
- tin trunk ▪ wet and dry emery paper for metalwork ▪ newspapers to protect your work area ▪ face mask ▪ large can of metal primer spray paint ▪ scrap paper ▪ large can of brown enamel aerosol paint ▪ spray mount ▪ large can of a cream-coloured enamel aerosol paint ▪ clear varnish and brush

1 Clean the trunk and rub down the surface with wet and dry emery paper. Pay particular attention to any areas that are chipped or flaking, rubbing the edges down well so that they blend into the adjoining paintwork. Roughen up the whole surface to give the primer a surface it can key into.

2 Protect the area with newspaper. Put on the face mask and apply the metal primer. Build it up in light even coats to avoid paint runs. Leave until completely dry. Tear the paper into strips. Use your eye to measure the width and don't try to do the job too neatly. Tear into smaller pieces.

3 Wear the face mask and apply the brown spray paint. When dry, apply the paper shapes. A light coating of spray mount will keep them in place. Start the pattern in the middle of a surface and work outwards leaving narrow pathways between each piece. Smooth the shapes with a roller.

4 Once the whole trunk has a covering of paper shapes, put on the face mask again and apply the cream spray paint all over the trunk.

5 Try to wait until the paint has dried before you remove the shapes to reveal the trunk's new African character – almost genuine giraffe! Enamel paint is pretty tough but you can add further protection with a coat of clear varnish.

Keeping clean!

Spray paints can be very messy because the paint drifts away into the air. If possible, use spray paints outside, but otherwise be prepared to cover a very wide area with newspaper in order to keep the rest of your home paint-free!

easy accessories

funky frames

Walls look awfully bare without any pictures, but not many people can afford original works of art – this project provides a good alternative. Frames can do so much more than protect your pictures and photographs. They can make an artistic statement of their own with the added bonus of sharing some creative family fun as you put them together and choose the best images to display in them.

the wine-lover's frame

If you have ever bothered to examine corks you cannot have failed to have notice how pretty they are – and that's not the drink talking! Each wine has a different cork with lettering, numerals, or an illustration of a bunch of grapes or another symbol indicating where it has come from.

Sadly, some wine bottles are now fitted with characterless reconstituted cork stoppers, or even plastic ones, so it really is our duty to save the genuine article and make something of it. We had a tough time collecting all these, especially the champagne corks for the corner pieces, but we did it all for the sake of our art. We advise you to do the same.

you will need:
■ old picture frame ■ sandpaper ■ loads of corks (ask a local restaurant or wine bar to save you an evening's worth if you are a slow drinker!) ■ glue gun or strong glue stick

1 Rub the frame down with sandpaper to give the glue a rough surface to grip onto.

2 Sort out the corks, choosing those with the best graphics.

3 Arrange the corks on the frame. Move them around until you are happy that you are making the most of them.

4 Lift them one at a time, apply the glue and stick them firmly in position.

5 Finish off with a champagne cork on each corner.

6 If you have a photograph of your chateau, this frame will set it off to perfection – if not, a bunch of plastic grapes looks pretty funky!

Getting funky

Jazzing up the accessories in a room is an easy way to change the look of a room. Simply painting your picture frames, or giving them a revamp as we have here, will give a whole new look at very little cost.

the stamp album frame

Stamps are miniature paintings that are easy to take for granted on their own, but they look fabulous when massed together. We found bags of pretty, but worthless, stamps in a junk shop and knew that they would look fabulous on an old black frame that we had languishing in our attic.

The frame had some surface damage that needed covering and these stamps were just the thing to make it look priceless. Check that the stamps you use are not rare or valuable – you don't want someone pointing out a valuable stamp once you have stuck it on a frame and varnished it!

you will need:
- lots of stamps ▪ PVA glue and coarse-haired brush
- old picture frame

1 Soak any stamps that are attached to paper in water so that they come away. Leave them upside down to dry.

the Monopoly® board frame

Does everyone else in the world manage to keep all the bits that you need to play a board game in the right place, or do all board games suffer the same fate as ours? Judging from all the games without their 'bits' that turn up in charity stores it seems that we are not alone. We used the famous Monopoly® board for our frame, but found many others that also look great, such as Cluedo® , snakes and ladders and ludo.

you will need:
- craft knife with straight steel edge ▪ games board
- hardboard ▪ square wooden frame ▪ wood glue (or any brand of PVA)
- panel pins ▪ hammer
- emulsion paint

1 Use the craft knife with the straight edge to cut away the centre section of the board.
2 Cut out a piece of hardboard as a backing for the frame.
3 Paint the hardboard bright red to match the red of the games board. If you are using another game choose a matching colour.

2 Coat the whole frame with PVA and leave it until touch dry.

3 In the meantime sort out your stamps into different colours, patterns and sizes.

4 Brush the stamps with PVA and arrange them on the frame.

5 Apply two coats of PVA to cover the whole frame. The PVA is milky when wet, but dries to a clear satin finish and will act as a protective varnish.

4 Glue the game border onto the wooden frame with wood glue or PVA.

5 Fix the hardboard onto the back of the frame with wood glue and panel pins.

6 Fill your frame! We found an old iron and sprayed it silver, and then made up some over-sized dice from leftover timber, decorating them with red paint and white sticker dots. Keep your ideas bold and on a large scale for a similar effect.

flower power pinboard frame

For this project you need bright fabric flowers with petals that have held their shape and colour. We used some we found on a Hawaiian fancy-dress costume. The drawing pins serve the dual purpose of forming the centres and keeping the flowers in place. For a more subtle effect use fake ivy or other fabric leaves around a frame and substitute staples for the drawing pins.

you will need:

- large old picture frame
- sandpaper ▪ white acrylic primer ▪ paint brushes
- acrylic paint ▪ hammer
- fabric flowers – try fancy-dress shops, milliners or haberdashers ▪ brightly coloured drawing pins
- piece of softboard to fit the frame or cork from an old pinboard ▪ panel pins and glue

1 Prepare the frame for painting by sanding it down and strengthening any wonky bits.

2 Apply a coat of white acrylic primer and leave to dry.

3 Paint the frame with your chosen acrylic paint. We used Indian red for the frame. Apply a second coat if required.

4 Decide on your flower arrangement. Aim for a balance of colours and shapes.

5 Place a drawing pin in the centre of each flower and attach to the frame. Use a small hammer if necessary. Incorporate a mixture of colours.

6 Cut out a piece of softboard to fit the frame and paint it a bright colour. We used ultramarine.

7 Fix it to the frame with panel pins and glue.

8 Fill the frame! We used it to display family photos, using more dressed-up drawing pins.

craft for kids

Kids will love getting crafty with junk – and when it costs you very little, everyone is happy! These projects are all easy but we suggest you keep an eye on things and help with cutting etc. And why not join in – craft is great stress-relief!

funky egg box anemones

This is a great project for those of us who cannot bear to throw out an egg box, and children will love it. It is easy, and compulsive enough to keep both kids and parents engrossed for hours.

Real anemones have an intense pure colour, and we find that watercolour inks recreate this well. If your egg boxes are coloured, we suggest you paint them white first. Opaque colour, such as poster paint, can be applied directly to any colour egg box.

you will need:

- egg boxes ▪ small scissors
- bendy drinking straws – fat milk-shake straws are best
- small can of black spray paint
- water-colour inks ▪ brush and water ▪ Blu-Tack ▪ black drawing pins ▪ green florist's tape

1 Cut the cups out of the egg box. Cut each one into four broad petal shapes, taking them down as far as the cup base.

2 Cut a fringe into the end of the drinking straw. Spray it black. Paint the flowers different colours, leaving a circle of white at the base.

74

3 Roll up a small ball of Blu-Tack and press this into the end of the straw to splay out the fringing. Push a black drawing pin into the Blu-Tack.

4 Use the scissors to poke a hole in the base of the egg cup. Thread the drinking-straw stem down through the hole, pulling it through until the flower centre is in place.

5 Stick the end of the green florist's tape onto the back of the flower and twist the stem until it is completely covered.

wire and button flowers

This project was inspired by a visit to a very funky craft shop in America where we saw a vase filled with brightly coloured old buttons threaded onto wire stems. We loved the simplicity of the idea, but couldn't resist taking it a step further by twisting the wire into different petal shapes.

We always investigate the contents of old biscuit tins in charity shops, and often find that they are full of all sorts of buttons. The colours, textures, shapes, patterns and weights are so diverse and, if we're lucky, we sometimes find a few that match.

you will need:

- loads of old buttons ▪ small long-nosed pliers
- galvanised garden wire

Method 1

1 Choose a gauge of wire that fits through the button holes, and is easy to bend yet strong enough to support the flower head. Green garden wire can also be used. Thread a wire through a button. Twist the wire to secure it around the stem.
2 Twist another strand of wire around the stem and then use the pliers to twist it into regular petal shapes.

Method 2

1 Find a piece of scrap wood and hammer in a circle of six or more nails with one in the centre.
2 Starting with a twist around the centre nail, run loops of wire around each of the outer nails keeping the petal shapes roughly the same shape and size.
3 Lift the flower off the nails and thread the wire up through one of the button holes, then back down through another to form the stem.

tin-can flowers

Clever can openers these days remove the whole lid from the can, leaving its edges sealed and safe – yet another piece of funky junk for us to play around with! Cans of fish, such as salmon and tuna, are the best for this project because they have imprinted numbers, names and ridges which add interest. Make sure you get creative with the nail varnish for extra funkiness!

you will need:

- several tin cans ▪ safety can opener ▪ selection of brightly coloured nail varnishes (or small pots of enamel paint)
- long-nosed pliers ▪ small hammer and panel pins ▪ bottle caps
- buttons ▪ galvanised wire – easy to bend but strong enough to take the weight of the bloom

1 Crimp the lids using the pliers. Repeat this action all around the lid to give it a corrugated surface.

2 Punch a hole in the centre with the hammer and panel pin. Then punch two holes in the bottle cap.

3 Thread a wire through the lid, one of the holes in the bottle cap and the button, then back down again through the other holes. Twist the two lengths of wire together to make the stem.

4 Without too much planning, launch yourself into the decoration of your flowers! Use different colours for the petals, and decorate with spots, stripes and zig-zags.

flower pots

Fish tank grit comes in funky colours and makes ideal soil!

you will need:
- clay flowerpots ▪ fish-tank grit ▪ sample pots of paint

1 Paint the outside of the clay pots, either plain or in striped patterns.

2 Half-fill the clay pot with grit, then arrange the flowers in it before filling it up. The grit will hold the flowers upright in the painted pot.

Flower arranging

Look out for some funky packaging in which to display your wire flowers. Italian olive oil or biscuit tins work very well, but there are many other brilliant designs to choose from.

cushions from clothes

Once you have grasped the idea that shirts, sweaters and cardigans have potential as cushion covers, it seems so glaringly obvious that you wonder why everyone doesn't recycle clothes this way. Cushions made from wool and velvet in particular command a very high price in up-market interiors shops.

One glance at the clothes rail in your local charity shop will reveal a wealth of styles to choose from: velvet or satin for the bedroom; florals for the garden; stripes or checks for the kitchen – just make a choice and get snipping and sewing.

cardi-cushions

Hand-knitted cushion covers usually come with very high price tags, but these look just as good at a fraction of the price. You can use any interesting Fair Isle, cable-stitch or stripy knits for cushions that are good to cuddle.

you will need:
- hand-knitted pullover or cardigan and matching wool ▪ tape measure ▪ webbing tape ▪ pins ▪ scissors or cutting wheel
- sewing machine ▪ darning needle

1 Measure from the bottom edge to under the arms of the cardigan and pin webbing tape to the outside of the knitting, making sure that the line is kept straight. Machine stitch the webbing in place.
2 Cut the knitting along the top edge of the webbing tape. If you use a cutting wheel, you will need to place a cutting mat beneath the knitting. Discard the arms and yolk of the cardigan or pullover.
3 Turn the knitting inside out. Use the matching wool and a darning needle to stitch up the top seams, working just inside the stitching on the webbing tape.
4 If you are converting a cardigan into a cushion cover, you can stitch up the bottom edge as well and unbutton the front to insert the cushion pad. If you are using a pullover, turn the cover the right way round and insert a cushion pad before sewing up.

plaid cushions

Some might call it sacrilege to cut up a designer shirt, but high-fashion clothes date quickly, with collars and cuts changing all the time. The shirts we chose had gone out of style, but the fabric was of high quality with a great plaid pattern in good colours. We sewed our shirts using French seams which are more complicated than ordinary seams but they are worth trying if you have the time as all the fraying edges are tucked away and the finish is very neat. We looked on this as a successful rescue mission.

you will need:

- brushed-cotton plaid shirt ▪ cushion pad
- pins ▪ scissors ▪ sewing machine
- matching thread ▪ iron and ironing board

1 Choose a cushion pad that will fit snugly inside the shirt. This cuts down on sewing as you can leave the existing side seams intact. Place it inside the buttoned-up shirt.
2 Place a row of pins along the top and bottom of the cushion to join the back and front of the shirt together.
3 Cut away and discard the rest of the shirt. Leave a 1.5cm/½in seam allowance beyond the pin line.
4 Use the sewing machine to stitch a straight seam along the pin line. Trim the fabric to within 1cm/¼in of the seam.
5 Turn the cushion cover inside out and press the seams flat.
6 Sew another line of stitching 1cm/¼in from the edge and then turn the cover the right way out. Press again.
7 Undo the buttons, put the cushion pad inside and button up!

speedy short-cuts

If you want to finish this project in five minutes flat and don't intend to look inside the cushion cover ever again, then don't bother with the French seam. Just turn the shirt inside out, stitch the two seams and turn it the right way around — and stuff it!

completely dotty lamp

Standard lamps fell from grace after the 1950s but you can still find them loitering about in the corners of second-hand shops, silently begging to be given a new lease of life. The one we found was quite sturdy with a broad, round base, bun feet and a turned shaft. It had been painted many times and looked scruffy, drab and un-remarkable. The lampshade was long-gone and probably just as well!

We decided that the lamp's time to shine had come and, after spending some time rubbing and scrubbing it, we gave it a bright new colour treatment and then covered it from head to toe in hundreds of stick-on spots. Our daughter Roxy was desperate to help and her little fingers did the job brilliantly.

We bought a new lampshade and painted it a wild ultramarine blue, before giving it a dotty makeover too. By the end of this project we were all seeing spots in front of our eyes. Stickers come in many shapes and sizes and this can take the strain out of pattern application. To prevent the edges from lifting and spoiling the effect, finish your lamp off with a coat of varnish.

you will need:

- sandpaper ▪ white spirit and cloth
- white acrylic primer ▪ paint brushes
- 4 bright emulsion or acrylic colours
- large plain lampshade ▪ adhesive dots in 6 different colours and three sizes – stationery shops sell these in packs or by the sheet
- clear gloss varnish and a new brush

1 Rub the old paintwork or varnish down with sandpaper. Using a cloth dampened with white spirit clean off the dust and eliminate any grease spots.

2 Paint the lamp base with the white acrylic primer. This will give an even matt surface and make sure that the top coat colours don't lose any of their brilliance.

3 Carefully paint all the large sections in your choice of colours. We used maroon, lime green and sunshine yellow. Pick out any features by painting them with darker colours. We used ultramarine blue.

4 Paint the lampshade. This is something you can do to change the colour of any lampshade using acrylic or emulsion paints. So easy!

5 Add dots to the lampshade in whatever design you like. Having fun is far more important than being neat! Varnish the whole lamp with clear gloss varnish using a clean brush.

practical matters

tools and equipment

A task is always much easier to perform when you have the perfect tool for the job, but these are often expensive items, and if you are just dabbling in woodwork, metal-work or paint effects it is useful to know a few shortcuts and tricks of the trade. You can have far more fun by spending some of your money on a basic set of tools, and the rest on junk in need of funk. Here we divide the tools up by task, so that you will be able to see what you need at a glance.

This is a really handy way of cleaning brushes that you've used for oil-based paint. Before use, drill a hole through the brush and then you'll be able to soak a brush as shown.

painting

- Medium (5cm/2in) household brush for covering large areas.
- Small (1.5cm/½in) brush for small areas.
- Set of inexpensive fine- and square-tipped artist's brushes for details such as lettering, stripes and other patterns.
- Mini-rollers and paint trays.
  - Foam rollers for oil-based paint such as gloss, satinwood and eggshell.
    - Medium-pile rollers for emulsion.
    - White spirit to clean off any oil-based paints.
    - Washing-up liquid to remove the last traces of water-based paint.

Brushes used for emulsion and acrylic paints should be rinsed under a running tap immediately. Oil-based paint will not harden if you stand the brushes in water until you are ready to clean them.

When a project calls for spray paint, buy it from a car-parts dealer where the prices are lowest. Cellulose thinners are the correct solvent for this type of paint.

cutting

- Tenon saw: good for most small timber-cutting jobs. This saw has a rigid strip along the back which assists in straight cutting, but will not go through timber any thicker than the depth of the blade.
- Hacksaw: has a fine blade ideal for cutting through metal.
- Jigsaw: a hand-held power tool with a vertical blade. Various blades available to suit different tasks and materials. This is a very useful and inexpensive power tool which enables you to make internal cuts by inserting the blade through a drilled hole, and to cut curves quickly and effortlessly.
- Chisel: needed to cut rebates for recessed hinges.
- Stanley knife: broad-handled knife with strong, replaceable blades.
- Scalpel or craft knife: for precision cutting of paper, fabric or cardboard shapes.
- Scissors: one small pair of nail scissors and one large pair of multi-purpose scissors.

general tools

- Scraper: for lifting mouldings and removing stripped paint.
- Clawhammer: for hammering in and pulling out nails.
- Small pein or cross-pein hammer: for panel and moulding pins.

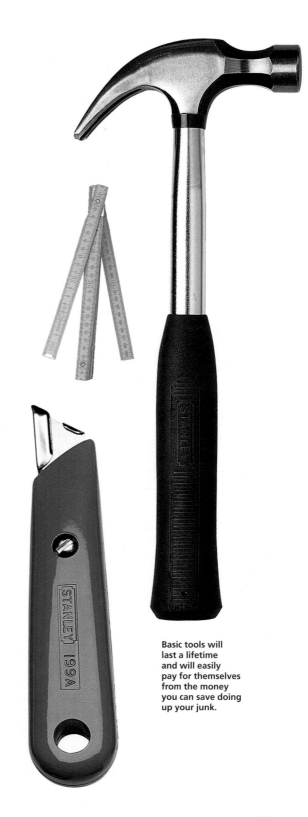

Basic tools will last a lifetime and will easily pay for themselves from the money you can save doing up your junk.

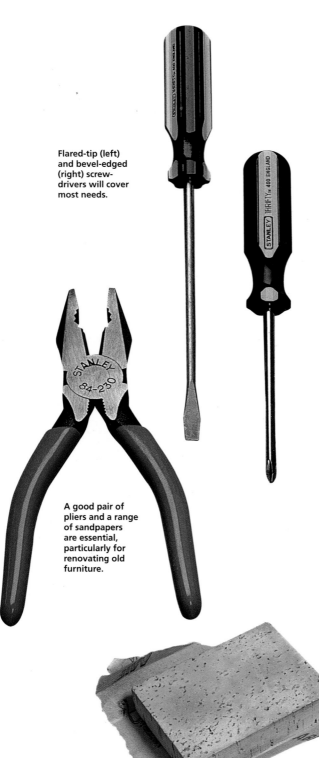

Flared-tip (left) and bevel-edged (right) screwdrivers will cover most needs.

A good pair of pliers and a range of sandpapers are essential, particularly for renovating old furniture.

- Set of screwdrivers: both flared-tip and bevel-edged type.
- Tape measure.
- Pliers: for pulling out old nails and twisting wire.

useful extras

- Set of G-clamps – for holding joints and other glued edges while they bond – cheap imported versions are fine.
- Power drill or screwdriver.
- Power sander: an orbital palm sander or finishing sander with dust bag.

general equipment

- Nails: ask for advice when you buy them so that you are sure to be using the ideal type for the job.
- Screws: brass, iron, stainless steel. Ask for advice about suitability when you buy them.
- Pins: panel pins, hardboard pins and moulding pins.
- Sandpaper: medium-grade for removing paint; fine-grade for finishing.
- Wet and dry emery paper: for rubbing down metal.
- Paint stripper: caustic liquid applied with a brush and removed with a scraper.
- Wire wool: medium- to fine-grade for removing stripped paint.
- Masking tape: choose a low-tack tape so you can remove it easily without taking paintwork with it.
- White spirit: for cleaning oil-based paints. Try to dispose of carefully, rather than pouring down a sink.

surface preparation

paint stripping

To assess which product will be best for the task at hand, scratch away the paint layers until you reach the bare wood. Chemical strippers come in various strengths, and you should aim to use the least environmentally harmful and most efficient product for the job.

Work in a well-ventilated area and protect the area with sheets of newspaper. Wear strong rubber gloves and safety goggles to protect your skin and eyes from the caustic solution.

you will need:
- chemical paint stripper ■ scraper ■ thick rubber gloves ■ safety goggles ■ wire wool ■ white spirit ■ cloth ■ newspapers

1 Following the instructions on the can, dispense some of the stripper into a glass jar and paint on a thick, even layer of the liquid or gel. Leave the solution in place for the suggested time or until the paint has blistered and crinkled. Use a scraper to move the softened paint, pushing the scraper away from you and cleaning the edge into a newspaper to be folded and bagged up for removal.
2 To remove the final sludgy paint, use a wire wool brush in white spirit and scrub it away.
3 The stripped surface can be sandpapered and then wiped with a sponge and warm water to remove any sawdust.
4 Use a cloth dipped in white spirit to remove final traces of dust, ready for a fresh coat of paint or varnish.

1

2

3

4

Use a piece of scrap wood or a cork block as a sanding block. It makes sanding much easier and more effective. Alternatively, invest in an electric sander.

Once your item of junk has been prepared (or 'keyed') it is ready for painting. A base coat will help prolong the life of the paintwork.

painted or varnished wood

If you want to paint over an already painted or varnished item, then follow these instructions. First check whether the painted or varnished surface is in good condition – if there are substantial areas where the paint or varnish has chipped off, you will get a better finish if you strip the paint completely (see previous page).

you will need:

- medium-grade sandpaper
- white spirit ▪ cloth

1 If you are repainting, then begin by wiping the surface down with a damp cloth, or washing it with soapy water if it is very dirty.

2 Use a medium-grade sandpaper to rub off the surface sheen to provide a rough surface for the paint to key to.

3 Wipe down with a cloth dampened with white spirit to remove any remaining traces of dust and grease.

4 Prime the surface with white acrylic primer. When dry, your surface is ready for painting.

laminates

Laminated surfaces are fashionable at the moment, and look great when repainted in the contemporary colours of today.

1 Scrub the surface with de-greasing soap. Then rub down with medium-grade sandpaper to scratch up the shiny surface.

2 Paint on a coat of tile primer, or spray with an enamel primer.

preparing rusty metal for painting

you will need:

■ wire brush ■ scraper ■ wet and dry emery
paper ■ white spirit ■ cloth ■ rust treatment
(optional)

1 Use a wire brush and get rid of any large
pieces of rust, then rub well with wire wool and
wet and dry emery paper until you can see the
gleam of bare metal.

2 Wipe away all the rust and dust using a cloth
dampened with white spirit. Whenever you
finish using solvents in this way, always unfold
the cloth to allow the residues to evaporate and
the fumes to disperse or soak it in water.
Bunched-up cloths have been known to
spontaneously combust!

3 If there was a lot of rust then it is wise to give
the cleaned-up metal and surrounding area a
paint-on rust treatment. This converts any
residual rust into hard metal and prevents new
rust from forming.

4 Prime with an aerosol enamel primer. Always
wear a face mask to prevent inhalation of
fumes and paint in a well-ventilated area,
preferably somewhere sheltered outdoors.
Spray paint drifts a long way, even in still
conditions, so make sure the surrounding area
is protected with newspaper or a dust sheet.

**A blow torch will
make light work
of paint-stripping.
If you have a large
area to strip, this
will be by far the
best way of
tackling the job.**

Removing nails is much easier than removing screws. Simply lever out using the reverse edge of a hammer head.

removing old screws

If screws are rusted and difficult to remove, make sure you are using the correct-sized screwdriver. Otherwise you will find it hard to get a firm grip on the screw.

Place your screwdriver in the screw slot, then tap it sharply with a hammer. This may be enough to loosen it. Otherwise surround the screw head with penetrating oil and leave for several hours. Alternatively, heat the screw head with a soldering iron. It will expand and then contract as it cools. If the screw head comes off and you cannot grip the shaft with pliers, fill the hole and re-site the screw.

re-gluing joints

you will need:

- scraper ▪ wood glue ▪ clamp or tape
- cloth ▪ panel pins and hammer

If you have found a chair or table with wobbly joints, do not despair. Wobbliness is usually the result of poor upholstering or misuse that has

If you want to repair more intricate joints, you are best advised to dismantle the piece of furniture before applying fresh glue.

weakened the joints. The problem isn't fatal –
re-gluing will usually be sufficient. If this still
doesn't work, a local carpenter should be able
to help, and still for less than a new chair.

1 Open the joint as wide as you can without
causing further damage.
2 Scrape off any old glue.
3 Apply a thin coating of wood glue to both
edges of the joint.
4 Press, then clamp or tape the joint. Wipe
away any excess glue with a damp cloth before
it sets to give a neat finish to the joint.
5 If possible tap in a panel pin or two to hold
the joint even more securely.

the right adhesive for the job

- Paper: PVA, wallpaper paste or glue stick.
Spray mount is removable for repositioning.
- Applied decorations: PVA, strong glue stick
e.g. UHU Powerstick, glue gun, or No More Nails.
- Wood: wood glue, glue gun or glue sticks.
- Metal: chemical metal or an epoxy resin glue.

To fix a wobbly chair leg, read the instructions above for
re-gluing joints.

If you don't have a clamp, thick masking tape will do to hold
glued joints together while the glue dries.

If you have a large area to fill, use a plastering tool.

filling holes and cracks

Filling holes and cracks in wood furniture is a quick way of improving the appearance of a piece. There are a wide range of wood fillers available which blend into the colour of the wood, which means you can even varnish for a natural wood finish.

1 Sand around the edges of the hole or crack.
2 Fill with all-purpose wood filler or flexible wood filler, pressing it deep into the hole. If the item is to be moved about or has any 'give' then use the flexible version.
3 When completely dry, sand the repair until it is level with the surrounding wood.

finishing touches

fitting new handles

A new set of handles can make all the difference. Old-fashioned hardware stores or smart new style emporiums are the places to look. Avoid DIY chains, unless you intend to revamp their cheapest wooden knobs or handles, because they only carry a very limited range. Choose your handles before you do up your piece of furniture as then the old holes can be filled and painted during the makeover.

Check that the shafts for fixing the handles are the right depth for your wood and that any protruding fixtures will not get in the way.

fitting new hinges
Remove the original hinges and take

New handles are one of the easiest and cheapest ways of giving junk a new lease of life.

one with you when looking for replacements. Different hinges work in different ways and you will need to replace yours with the same type. When fitting new hinges only fit one screw at a time, checking that the door still swings open and closes properly after each. Slightly worn hinges can be swapped over from top to bottom to correct a sagging door. Always make sure the screw heads are flush with the hinge or the door will not shut properly.

varnishing

A coat of varnish will give a hard protective coating and prevent all your hard work from being done in vain!

There are two main types:

■ Acrylic: water-based, quick-drying and suitable for indoors. Available in the following range:

Clear matt: invisible.

Clear satin: gives a slight sheen.

Clear gloss: leaves a shiny surface.

Tinted versions also available.

■ Polyurethane: a resin-based varnish suitable for indoors and out. It is hard-wearing but takes longer to dry and has a stronger odour than acrylic. Available in the same range as acrylic varnish.

Either use a clean brush or soft cloth for applying varnish. You can opt for a varnish to match the colour of your wood, or take it up a few tones for a new look. To keep your varnished wood looking good, wax regularly.

Use a clean brush or soft cloth for varnishing. Fill the brush or moisten the cloth and start by dabbing it in the centre of the area, then work it out towards the edges. When the whole surface is covered, drag a brush across in the

index

stockists and suppliers

We would like to extend big thanks to the following companies for supplying the materials we used in the projects:

Lakeland Limited – cleaning products and household goods
Alexandra Buildings
Windermere
Cumbria
LA23 1BQ
Telephone 01539 488 100

DeWalt Tools – professional range of power tools
210 Bath Road
Slough
Berkshire
SL13YD
Telephone 01753 567 055

Hamilton Acorn Limited – fine decorating products
Halford Road
Attleborough
Norfolk
NR17 2HZ
For names of suppliers telephone: 01953 453 201

Focus /Do it All Ltd – A leading D.I.Y. Superstore. Free Customer Helpline for advice on decorating projects, address of nearest store and product information. Call 0800 436 436.

acknowledgements

The authors would like to thank everyone involved in the making of the series *Funky Junk*. We also extend our thanks to Becky Humphreys at HarperCollins*Publishers* and Steve Differ for his lovely photographs.